CHARACTER EDUCATION

I Am
Respectful

by Jenny Fretland VanVoorst

BLASTOFF! READERS

BELLWETHER MEDIA · MINNEAPOLIS, MN

Note to Librarians, Teachers, and Parents:

Blastoff! Readers are carefully developed by literacy experts and combine standards-based content with developmentally appropriate text.

Level 1 provides the most support through repetition of high-frequency words, light text, predictable sentence patterns, and strong visual support.

Level 2 offers early readers a bit more challenge through varied simple sentences, increased text load, and less repetition of high-frequency words.

Level 3 advances early-fluent readers toward fluency through increased text and concept load, less reliance on visuals, longer sentences, and more literary language.

Level 4 builds reading stamina by providing more text per page, increased use of punctuation, greater variation in sentence patterns, and increasingly challenging vocabulary.

Level 5 encourages children to move from "learning to read" to "reading to learn" by providing even more text, varied writing styles, and less familiar topics.

Whichever book is right for your reader, Blastoff! Readers are the perfect books to build confidence and encourage a love of reading that will last a lifetime!

This edition first published in 2019 by Bellwether Media, Inc.

No part of this publication may be reproduced in whole or in part without written permission of the publisher. For information regarding permission, write to Bellwether Media, Inc., Attention: Permissions Department, 6012 Blue Circle Drive, Minnetonka, MN 55343.

Library of Congress Cataloging-in-Publication Data

Names: Fretland VanVoorst, Jenny, 1972- author.
Title: I Am Respectful / by Jenny Fretland VanVoorst.
Description: Minneapolis, MN : Bellwether Media, Inc., 2019. |
   Series: Blastoff! Readers: Character Education | Includes bibliographical references and index.
Identifiers: LCCN 2018033425 (print) | LCCN 2018034232 (ebook) |
   ISBN 9781681036540 (ebook) | ISBN 9781626179295 (hardcover : alk. paper) |
   ISBN 9781618915009 (pbk. : alk. paper)
Subjects: LCSH: Respect for persons–Juvenile literature.
Classification: LCC BJ1533.R42 (ebook) | LCC BJ1533.R42 F74 2019 (print) | DDC 179/.9–dc23
LC record available at https://lccn.loc.gov/2018033425

Editor: Christina Leaf   Designer: Jeffrey Kollock

Printed in the United States of America, North Mankato, MN

Table of Contents

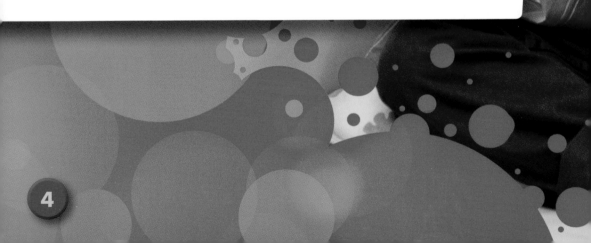

What Is Respect?

Your brother is watching a show. But you want to watch something else.

Do you **interrupt** him?
Or are you respectful?

Respectful people treat others well. They **value** others' needs and wants.

Respectful people
have good **manners**.
They are **polite**
and **patient**.
They follow the rules.

Why Be Respectful?

People know you value them when you show respect.

Respect helps **relationships** work smoothly. It is hard to get along with others without respect.

Who Is Respectful?

You Are Respectful!

It is easy to
show respect!
Use good manners.
Listen when
others speak.

Treat others how you would like to be treated.

Respectful people
make the best friends!

Glossary

interrupt

to stop an activity or event

polite

well-mannered

manners

the way people act

relationships

ties between people

patient

able to wait without becoming upset

value

to find to be important

To Learn More

AT THE LIBRARY

Murray, Julie. *Respect*. North Mankato, Minn.:
ABDO Kids, 2018.

Ponto, Joanna. *Being Respectful*. New York,
N.Y.: Enslow Publishing, 2016.

Raatma, Lucia. *Respect*. Ann Arbor, Mich.:
Cherry Lake Publishing, 2014.

ON THE WEB

FACTSURFER

Factsurfer.com gives you
a safe, fun way to find
more information.

1. Go to www.factsurfer.com.

2. Enter "respect" into the search box.

3. Click the "Surf" button and select your book
   cover to see a list of related web sites.

Index

The images in this book are reproduced through the courtesy of: wavebreakmedia, front cover; John T, pp. 2-3, 22-24; monkeybusinessimages, pp. 4-5, 6-7; Suzanne Tucker, pp. 8-9; Monkey Business Images, pp. 10-11, 22 (middle right); JGalione, pp. 12-13; imtmphoto, pp. 14-15; Photographee.eu, p. 15 (good, bad); FatCamera, pp. 16-17; FamVeld, pp. 18-19; Svitlana Bezuhlova, pp. 20-21; Dmytro Zinkevych, p. 22 (top left); michaeljung, p. 22 (middle left); Romrodphoto, p. 22 (bottom left); Viacheslav Nikolaenko, p. 22 (top right); Melle V, p. 22 (bottom right).